This Book Belongs To:

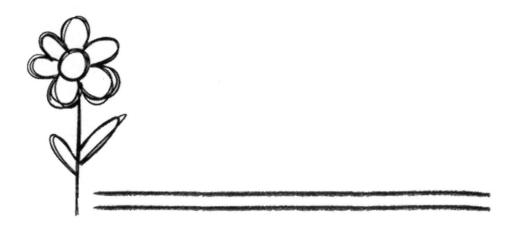

Prevent Bleeding

With Amazon paper selection, certain coloring pens and markers will bleed through. The best way to prevent bleeding is to place one or two scrap papers behind the pages you're about to color.
Thank you for understanding!

Our Coloring Community

Join our group and share your artwork with other artist!

Connect on Social Media

Scan the QR code to visit our social media where we upload relaxing coloring videos regularly.

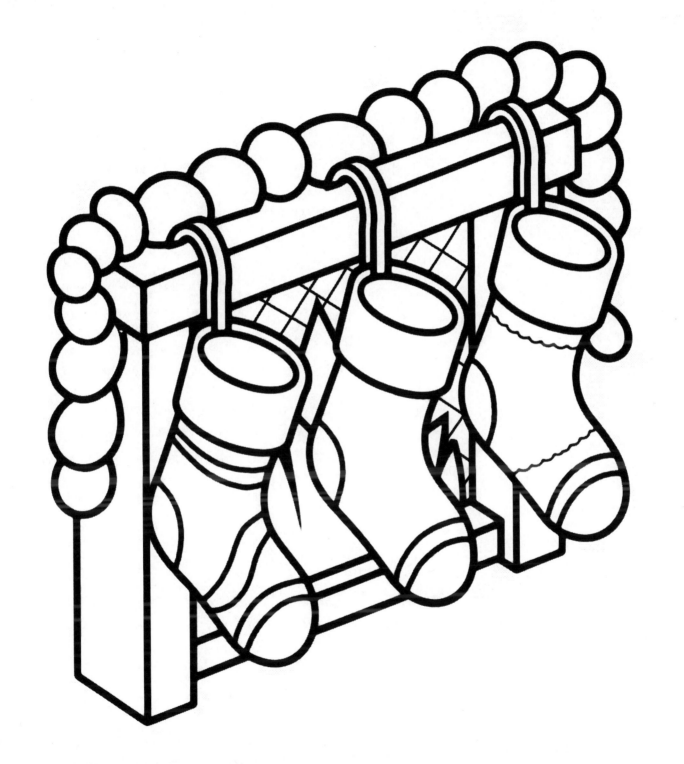

11/15/24 Friday

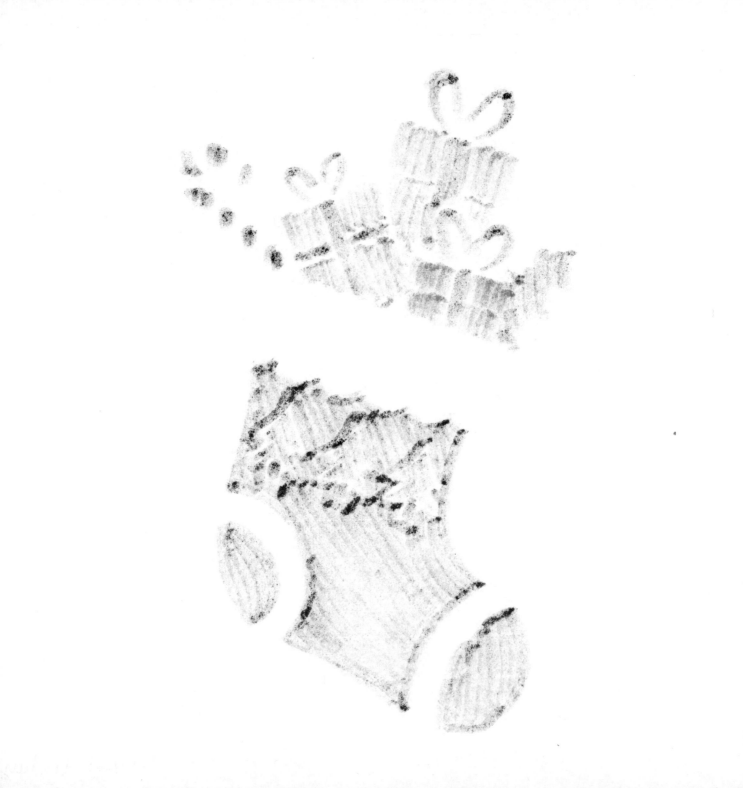

We hope you're enjoying your recent purchase from us! Your feedback helps us grow and ensures we're delivering top-notch products to amazing customers like you.

💬 **Share your thoughts:**
How did the product meet your expectations?
We're all about honest reviews
— good, bad, or somewhere in between.

📷 **A picture's worth a thousand words:**
Feel free to snap a pic of your new purchase!
We'd love to see your artistic work.

To leave a review, just head over to our product page on Amazon and let your thoughts flow. Your time and input mean the world to us, and we can't wait to hear what you have to say.

39947468R00057